THE NEW **anchor** BOOK OF
Crewel Stitches and Patte

D1380318

rles
don

Compiled by Eve Harlow

Contents

Introduction

Crewel is one of the oldest English Embroidery techniques and, along with other forms of needlework, is enjoying a revival.

This new book of crewel embroidery stitches will, therefore, be of interest to anyone who loves embroidery, not just teachers and students, but to needlewomen everywhere.

You will find familiar stitches here, perhaps with new ways of working them. You will also find stitches that were popular for crewel embroidery in the seventeenth century.

The stitches are set out in alphabetical order so that you can quickly locate a particular stitch and, at the back of the book, some of the designs are given as trace-off patterns for you to work yourself.

Basque Stitch

This is one of the knot or loop stitches, which are useful when a raised texture is required in a pattern. In the design on the opposite page, 'Blue Bee', the stitch is used to decorate the flowing leaf motif behind the oak leaf, and the leaf shape in the bottom right corner. Satin Stitch, Back Stitch, Chain Stitch and Trellis Stitch are also used in the design.

A warm and rich range of Stranded Cotton colours has been used as follows: 06, 09, 011, 326, 9575, 5975, 311, 885, 848, 849 and 850.

Delicate interpretation of leaves, sprays and flowers such as 'Blue Bee' is typical of designs of the eighteenth century, and motifs like this would have been used on large pieces of embroidery, such as wall hangings and bed hangings.

Fig 1 *Bring the thread through at A and insert the needle at B, thread behind the needle. Bring needle through at C, below B, thread forward and under needle.*

Fig 2 *Re-insert needle immediately below at D, and under thread loop, emerging at E, between A and B, keeping needle under loop of thread.*

Fig 3 *Continue working in this way, spacing stitches evenly. To complete the last stitch, insert the needle at F, level with E.*

Blue Bee ▶
A trace-off pattern for this design is on page 98

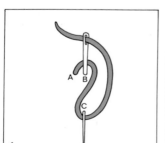

1

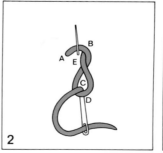

2

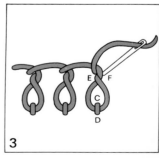

3

Battlemented Couching

To work this stitch, four sets of vertical and horizontal threads are laid, one set of four on the other. The stitch is traditionally worked in either light to dark tones or the reverse but for clarity the diagrams do not follow this but are shown in contrast colours.

The stitch has been used for the large leaf in the centre of the design 'Hedgerow' on the opposite page, together with Satin Stitch, Long and Short Stitch, French Knots, Chain Stitch, Back Stitch, Fly Stitch, Filled Stem Stitch and Daisy Stitches.

Fig 1 Work vertical stitches A-B, C-D, E-F. Then work horizontal stitches G-H, I-J, K-L. Keep all stitches equidistantly spaced.

Fig 2 The second stage stitches are worked to the right of stitches A-B, C-D, E-F, and above stitches G-H, I-J, K-L. Keep stitches parallel and touching.

Fig 3 Lay two more sets of stitches in the same way. Tie down the last set of stitches where they cross by working a small diagonal stitch from right to left.

Fig 4 Work a small tying stitch at each intersection as shown.

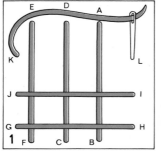

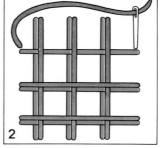

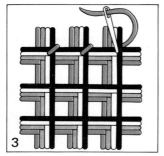

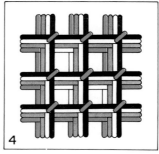

Hedgerow ▶

Brick and Cross Filling

Large leaves always present a challenge in crewel work and offer many opportunities for inspired use of filling stitches. In the fern-like leaf motif on the opposite page, with a small insect about to land, the main area of the leaf has been worked in Brick and Cross Filling, with Stem Stitch outlining. Other stitches include Chain Stitch, Buttonhole Stitch, Cretan Stitch, Satin Stitch and French Knots.

Fig 1 Work blocks of 5 horizontal satin stitches, the stitches touching. The width of the space between blocks should be the same as the width of the blocks. The depth of the space between the rows of blocks should be the same as the depth of a block.

Fig 2 To work a Cross between blocks, bring the thread through at A and insert the needle at B, bringing it out at C.

Fig 3 Complete the Cross by inserting the needle at D, then bring it out half-way along A-B, at E.

Fig 4 Insert the needle at F to couch down the Cross stitch.

Fig 5 shows the finished effect.

Fern ▶

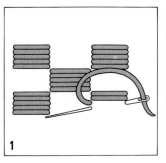

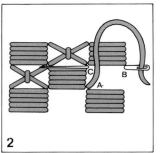

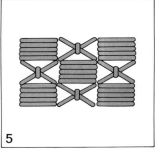

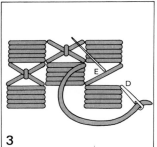

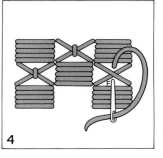

6

Brick Satin Filling

Small mounds or little hills often appear at the base of crewel work designs, especially when a tree or a large shrub is the central part of the design. You will sometimes find flowers and leaves tucked between the mounds or, as in the design 'Oak Tree' on the opposite page, a small animal, such as a rabbit. Rabbits were popular in crewel designs and this might have been because 'bunny' was a term of affection for girls in the late seventeenth century.

Tree trunks must be handled carefully because, by their size alone, they can easily dominate a design. A related range of green and ochre tones has been used for the tree here, and the strength of the scheme has been offset by the beautiful shading of the falling leaf. Stranded Cotton has been used to work the design.

Fig 1 A row: *Work 4 straight stitches to the same length, touching, and following the design line on the top edge. To the right, work 4 short straight stitches to just under half the length, stitches touching and following the design line on the top edge. Continue, working 4 long and then 4 short stitches.*

Fig 2 B row: *Work 4 long straight stitches immediately under those of A row, and to the same length. Work 4 long straight stitches of the same length under the short stitches of A row. Continue to the end of row B.*

Fig 3 C row: *Work 4 short straight stitches immediately under the long straight stitches of row B. Work 4 long stitches immediately below the long stitches of row B. Continue across the row. If the pattern is to be continued to fill a shape, repeat rows A, B and C again.*

Oak Tree ▶

A trace-off pattern for this design is on page 99

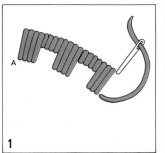 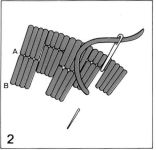 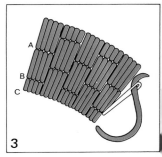

Burden Stitch

This is a form of couched work where first blocks of thread are laid and then the couching stitches are worked. In the charming design opposite, 'Squirrel', the stitch has been used to work the mounds in the foreground in brown, green and cream Tapisserie wools. The squirrel is worked in Stranded Cotton in Long and Short Stitch so that light catches the threads, providing texture interest among the matt areas of Tapisserie wools. Stranded Cotton has also been used to work the acorns spray.

Acorns often appear in crewel designs and provide good opportunities for splashes of colour or stitch texture.

Stranded Cotton colours are as follows: 0884, 0883 and 0366. Tapisserie wools are 0722, 0240, 0265, 0266, 0358, 0899, 3229 and 010.

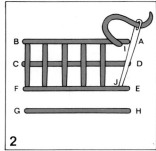

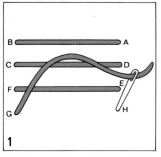

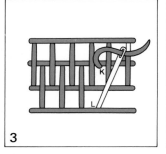

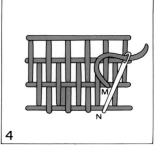

Fig 1 *Work horizontal stitches, A-B, C-D, E-F, G-H. Keep stitches equidistant.*

Fig 2 *Work vertical stitches between A-B and E-F, taking stitches over C-D (see I-J being worked).*

Fig 3 *Work vertical stitches between C-D and G-H, taking stitches over E-F (see K-L being worked).*

Fig 4 *To complete the stitch, work vertical stitches between E-F and G-H, taking stitches over G-H (see M-N being worked).*

Squirrel ▶
A trace-off pattern for this design is on page 100

10

Buttonhole Block Shading

Here is another way of handling a large leaf area in a design with rows of Buttonhole Block Shading in a range of related blue and blue-green tones.

Stranded Cotton has been used to work the design as follows: 968, 969, 970, 048, 162, 161, 168, 167, 185 and 213.

Fig 1 *Bring the thread through at A and insert the needle at B, bringing it out at C, thread under needle.*

Fig 2 *Make the second Buttonhole Stitch by inserting the needle at D and bringing it out at E, thread under needle.*

Fig 3 *Continue in the same way to complete a row of Buttonhole Stitch.*

Fig 4 *Work a second row of Buttonhole Stitch immediately above the first.*

Fig 5 *The diagram shows the stitch worked to follow a curved design line, as in 'Peony' opposite.*

Peony ▶
A trace-off pattern for this design is on page 101

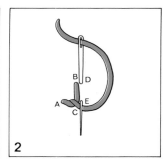

1

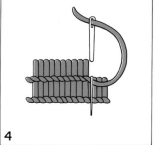

2

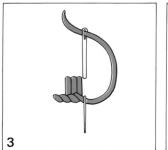

3

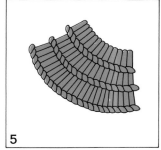

4

5

Buttonhole, German Knotted

Five different stitch combinations have been used to work the leaves of the 'tree' in the design on the opposite page. This is an ideal design for developing filling stitch possibilities and it has also broken away from the usual rather naturalistic colourings.

Stranded Cotton has been used in the embroidery as follows: colour numbers 0292, 0301, 0302, 0305, 0314, 0886, 0887, 0888 and 0906.

The design could be used for corner motifs for a rectangular fire screen with small sprays of flowers, leaves and berries in the same range of colours, scattered over the main area.

Stitches used in the design are Stem Stitch, Satin Stitch, Chevron Stitch, Chain and Back Stitches, Buttonhole Stitch and Trellis Stitch.

Fig 1 *Make a regular Buttonhole Stitch by bringing the thread through at A, inserting the needle at B and bringing it out at C, thread under needle.*

Fig 2 *Work the second Buttonhole Stitch D-E, then pass the needle under the*

threads of both stitches.

Fig 3 *Bring the thread round and pull gently, then insert the needle at F ready to make the first Buttonhole Stitch of the next group, F-G. Keep groups of stitches equidistantly spaced.*

Orange Tree ▶

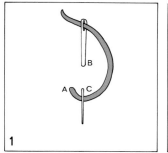

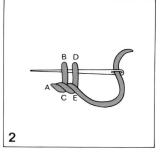

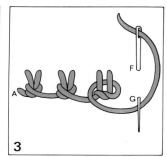

14

Open and Knotted Buttonhole

This is one of the fillings known as ground-covering stitches.

Fig 1 Stitches can be worked over a row of Back Stitches or over a laid thread.

Fig 2 Work even Buttonhole Stitches over a laid thread as shown without piercing fabric. Do not pull stitches tightly

Fig 3 For the second row, attach the thread at the right and work loose stitches into the loops of the previous row.

Fig 4 Shows three rows worked.

Fig 5 To work the Knotted variation, pass the needle from left to right behind the stitch just made as shown. When working the second row of stitches, the needle is passed from right to left behind the stitch.

Fig 6 Shows three rows of the stitch.

Blue Flower ▶

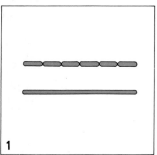

1

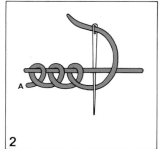

2

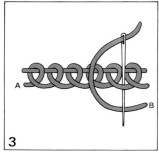

3

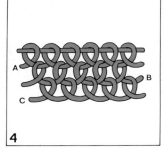

4

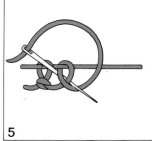

5

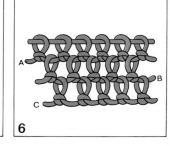

6

16

Buttonhole Scale Filling

This attractive filling stitch is, as its name suggests, rather like fish scales in effect. The scales can be worked to varying depths and widths, to fill a space and some scales can be left unworked for textural interest. The effect of the stitch is heightened by the use of related colours.

Fig 1 Bring the thread through at A and insert the needle at B, bringing it out at C, thread under needle, to make the first Buttonhole Stitch.

Fig 2 Insert the needle at D, beside B and following the curved design line. Bring the needle through at E, thread under needle, beside C, and following the curved design line.

Fig 3 Continue working Buttonhole Stitches in the same way, varying the length of stitches, keeping them close together at the top end, so that the knots follow the curve of the design line.

Fig 4 The 'scales' of the design are followed, the knots of the Buttonhole stitches overlapping the stitches of previous rows.

Fig 5 This shows the effect of the overlapping 'scales'.

Blue Poppy ▶

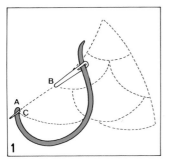

1

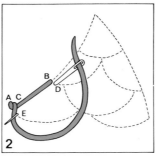

2

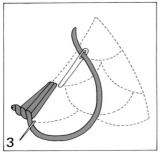

3

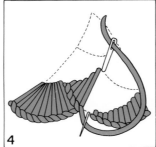

4

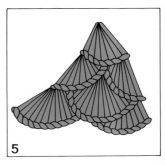

5

18

Buttonhole Square Filling

This attractive filling stitch can be varied by working varying numbers of stitches in the blocks, as shown in the design on the opposite page. The diagrams, however, show the stitch worked in groups of three stitches. Small single stitches can be worked to further vary the effect — French Knots and Detached Chain Stitches are illustrated.

The design, 'Blue Leaves', uses a limited range of Stranded Cotton colours on a blue satin-finished embroidery fabric and this scheme might be used for an attractive cushion cover, sprays repeated and set at different angles to cover the area.

Thread colours are as follows: 0875, 0876, 0878, 0399, 0977 and 0978.

Fig 1 *Work Buttonhole Stitches in groups of 3 as shown with space between the groups.*

Fig 2 *For the second row of the Filling, work Buttonhole Stitches just above the middle of the edge of the stitches of the previous row.*

Fig 3 *Filling with Knot: work a French Knot in the spaces between groups of Buttonhole Stitches.*

Fig 4 *Filling with Daisy: work a single Detached Chain Stitch in the spaces between groups of Buttonhole Stitches.*

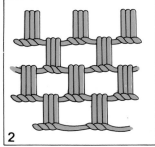

1

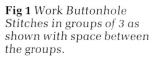

2

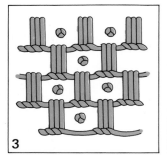

3

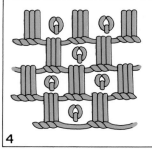

4

20

Blue Leaves ▶

Buttonhole Triangle Filling

Fig 1 Bring the thread through at A and insert the needle at B, diagonally to the right, and bring it out at C to make a sloping Buttonhole Stitch.

Fig 2 Insert the needle at B again and bring it out at D, a short distance from C.

Fig 3 Work 5 Buttonhole Stitches, all worked from B and spacing the knots so that a triangle is formed. Begin the next triangle by inserting the needle the width of the triangle base from B, bringing it out with the thread under the needle, ready to make the first Buttonhole Stitch of the next group of 5 stitches.

Fig 4 Two triangles worked.

Fig 5 Set the third triangle above triangles one and two.

Fig 6 Continue in the same way, working groups of triangles to fill the design space.

Lilac ▶

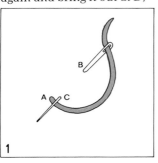

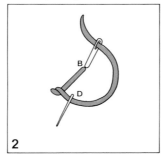

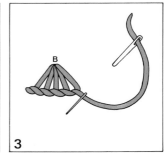

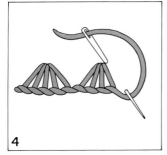

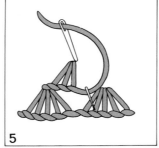

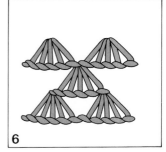

Up and Down Buttonhole

This stitch can be used as a filling stitch, worked in rows to fill shapes, or used in single rows following a curved design line, when the stitch can help to give 'lightness' to the design.

Stranded Cotton colours are 0259, 0260, 0261, 0262, 9575, 5975, 0361, 0362, 0363 and 0365.

Fig 1 *Bring the thread through at A and insert the needle at B, bringing it out at C, close by A, thread under needle.*

Fig 2 *Pull through and insert the needle at D, close to C and take a straight upward stitch, coming out at E, close to B, keeping thread under needle as shown.*

Fig 3 *Pull through gently, first in an upward movement then downwards. Insert the needle at F, bring out at G, leaving a space between E-D.*

Fig 4 *Work H-I to complete second group of stitches.*

Fig 5 *Three pairs of stitches are shown here with the first stitch of the fourth pair being worked (J-K).*

Nosegay ▶

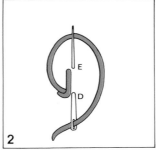

1

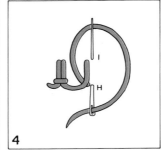

2

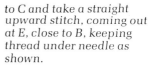

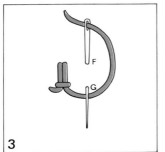

3

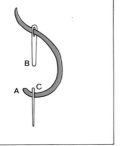

4

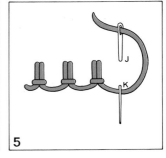

5

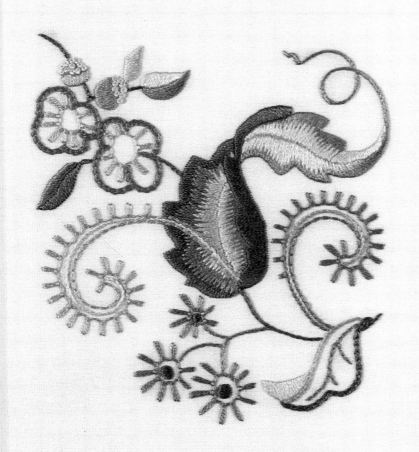

Chain Stitch Filling

In the design on the opposite page, 'Flower Tree', different treatments have been used for the leaves. The design is, therefore, an ideal practice project for a beginner in crewel embroidery. The trace-off pattern is given on pages 102 and 103.

Shaded Chain Stitch Filling has been used for leaves. Battlemented Couching is used for the large, fruit-like area near to the top of the design and a realistic four-petalled flower is worked in Long and Short Stitch. Long and Short Stitch is also used for one of the mounds below

the 'Flower Tree', with another in open Buttonhole Stitch and French Knots. Back Stitch, Coral Stitch and Stem Stitch are used to work tendrils.

Stranded Cotton is used for the embroidery.

Fig 1 *Outline the design shape with Chain Stitches.*

Fig 2 *Work the next row inside the outline, working stitches so that they touch.*

Fig 3 *Continue working Chain stitch rows inside the outline to fill the shape.*

Flower Tree ▶
Trace-off patterns for this design are on pages 102 and 103

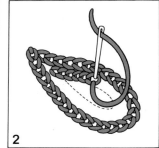

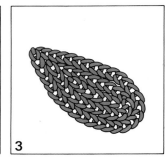

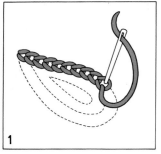

Chain Outline

Fig 1 Bring the thread through at A at the top of the design line. Holding the thread down with the thumb, insert the needle a thread away from A.

Fig 2 Holding the thread down with the thumb, bring the needle through at B.

Fig 3 Pull through gently and, holding the thread down with the thumb, insert the needle again a thread away from B.

Fig 4 Bring the needle through at C, the loop of thread under the needle, holding it down with the thumb.

Fig 5 Still holding the thread down with the thumb, insert the needle again at C, a thread away.

Fig 6 Continue in the same way, following the design line and keeping the loops of the chain as even as possible. Fasten the last loop with a small stitch.

Purple Parrot ▶
A trace-off pattern for this design is on page 104

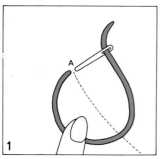

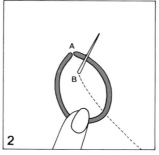

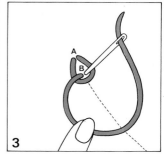

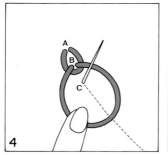

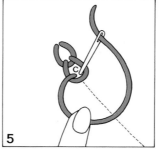

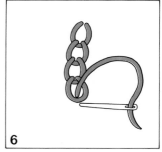

Twisted Chain, Detached Chain

Fig 1 Bring the thread through at A, hold it down with the thumb, insert the needle a little to the left at B, take a small slanting stitch across the line of the design (keeping the thread under the needle point) and bring the needle out at C.

Fig 2 Pull the thread up to form a twisted chain, hold it down with the thumb, insert the needle at D and bring it out at E.

Fig 3 Pull the thread through to form a twisted chain and then continue, following the sequence.

Detached Twisted Chain:
Fig 4 Bring the thread through at A and work the stitch as Fig 1 but take a longer slanting stitch B-C.

Fig 5 Bring the thread out at C and make a small stitch over the loop, inserting the needle at D to secure the stitch.

Fig 6 Detached Twisted Chain stitches can be scattered for a filling.

Leaf ▶

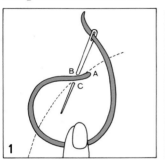

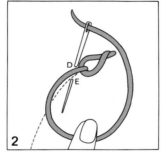

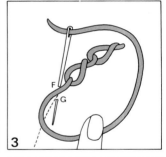

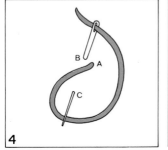

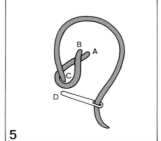

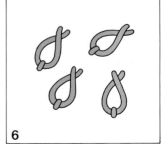

Chessboard Filling

This is a traditional crewel embroidery filling stitch and is often found in old embroideries. Satin Stitch blocks are worked alternating with spaces of the same size. The Filling is finished with a Cross in a contrasting colour. The effect can be seen in the large flower form in the design on the opposite page.

Fig 1 Work straight vertical stitches in groups of 5 stitches to form blocks.

Fig 2 The spaces between blocks should be the same size as the blocks themselves. Having worked the fifth stitch of the block, bring the thread through at top left and insert the needle at bottom right, bringing it out at bottom left of the block.

Fig 3 To complete a cross over the block, insert the needle at top right and bring it out midway along the diagonal stitch, passing the needle under that stitch.

Fig 4 Tie the cross by making a small vertical stitch over the centre.

Fig 5 This shows a group of 5 blocks each worked with a cross.

Flower and Snail ▶
A trace-off pattern for this design is on page 105

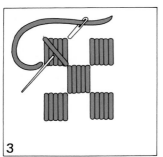

1

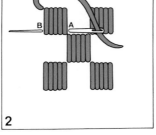

2

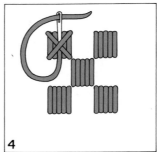

3

4

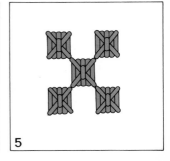

5

Half Chevron

Based on the Chevron Stitch, this pretty variation can be worked in straight rows or can be worked to follow curved design lines. The effect can be seen in the design on the opposite page 'Purple Blossom' where Half Chevrons are used for the seeds in the flower centre and also for the mound under the flower 'tree'.

Fig 1 Bring the thread through at A on the lower design line, insert the needle at B and take a small stitch, bringing the needle out at C (half way between A and B). Keep the thread below the needle.

Fig 2 Insert the needle at D on the upper design line, take a small stitch and bring the needle out at E, keeping thread under needle.

Fig 3 Insert the needle at F on the lower design line with the thread above the needle, bring it out at B.

Fig 4 Insert the needle at G and take a small stitch, bringing it out at F.

Fig 5 This shows the effect of a row of Half Chevron Stitches.

Purple Blossom ▶
A trace-off pattern for this design is on page 106

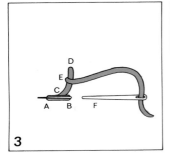

1

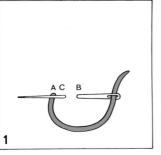

2

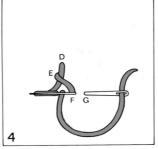

3

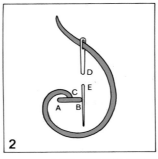

4

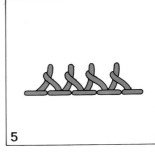

5

Cloud Filling

Cloud Filling is one of the weaving stitches and is rather like Wave Stitch in effect. Several rows of small, vertical stitches are laid then a contrasting colour thread is worked through. The effect can be seen in the design on the opposite page 'Pears', where the stitch has been used to fill the leaves.

Other stitches in the embroidery are Long and Short Stitch, Satin Stitch, Stem Stitch and shaded Chain Stitches.

Stranded Cotton has been used throughout on a satin-finished cotton embroidery fabric.

Fig 1 *Lay several rows of small vertical stitches in an alternating pattern as shown.*

Fig 2 *Using a tapestry needle and yarn or thread, work strands through the laid stitches, A to B to C to D to E.*

Fig 3 *For the second row of threaded strands, work through F to A to G to C to H to E to I, thus forming 'cloud' shapes. Continue, working from F through J to G to K to H to L to I. Continue threading until all the Back Stitches have been worked.*

Fig 4 *This shows the effect of the Filling.*

1

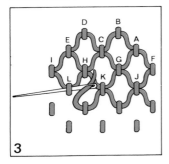

2

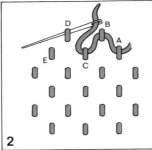

3

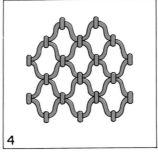

4

36

Pears ▶

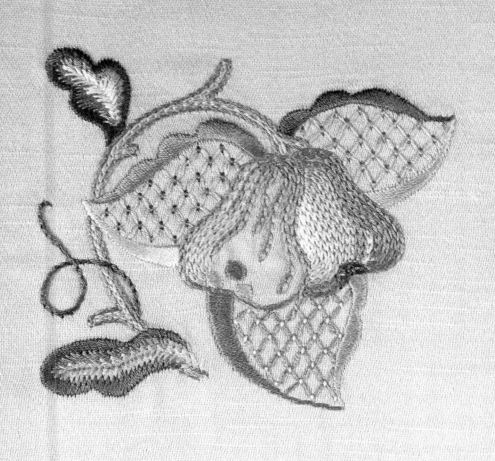

Coral Stitch

This is one of the group of stitches known as knot stitches and is usually used as a simple outline stitch with knots along the row. It is often used to work stems and twigs but is also a particularly effective filling stitch, when contrasting texture is required. The stitch has been used extensively in interpreting the design 'Blossom' on the opposite page, the flower petals contrasting with the smoothness of Satin Stitch. Stranded Cotton has been used for the embroidery as follows: colours 095, 0120, 0121, 0122, 0158, 0847, 0848, 0849, 0850, 0869, 0870, 0871, 0872, 0873.

Fig 1 Bring the thread through at A and, holding the thread down with the thumb, insert the needle just above the thread at B. Take a small stitch on the design line and bring the needle out at C. The thread goes over the needle and then under it as shown.

Fig 2 Pull through gently and work in the same way, D-E, for the next knot. Work knots at small, regular intervals.

Fig 3 Coral Knot is shown here as an outline stitch. If knots are worked closer together an interesting texture is achieved see 'Blossom' opposite.

Fig 4 Rows of Coral Knots worked close together as a filling.

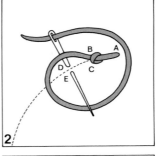

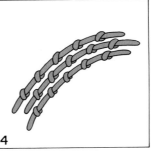

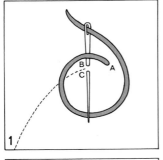

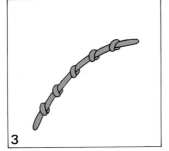

Blossom ▶
A trace-off pattern for this design is on page 107

38

Cretan Stitch, Open and Closed

Fig 1 For a leaf form, bring the thread through at A at the apex of the shape. Insert the needle at B on the upper side and take a small vertical stitch to C, with the thread looped under the needle.

Fig 2 On the bottom side, take a small stitch from D to E, with the thread looped under the needle. The stitches B-C and D-E should be the same length.

Fig 3 Insert the needle at F and make a small stitch bringing the needle through at G.

Fig 4 Insert the needle at H and make a small stitch bringing the needle through at I.

Fig 5 This shows the effect of Open Cretan.

Fig 6 Closed Cretan is worked in the same way but stitches are set close together.

High Summer ▶

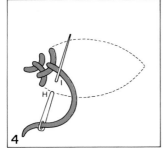

1

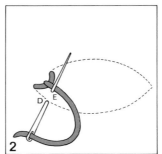

2

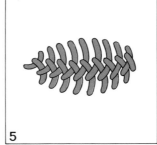

3

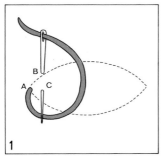

4

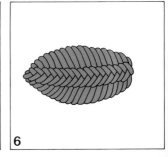

5

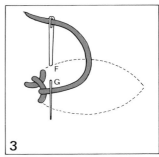

6

Detached Chain Stitch (Daisy)

This well-known and popular embroidery stitch is used extensively in crewel work, often for seeding when a stronger design effect is required. In the design on the opposite page, Leaf, Detached Chain Stitches are used to provide both colour and texture, so that the autumn leaf appears to be catching the light.

This design would be ideal for working along a curtain hem or for a pair of tie-backs.

Fig 1 Bring the thread through at A and, holding the thread down with the thumb, insert the needle again at A, a single thread away.

Fig 2 Still holding the loop of thread, bring the needle through at B.

Fig 3 Pull through gently until a rounded chain is formed then tie the stitch by making a small stitch over the loop at C.

Fig 4 The thread can be secured on the wrong side with a small Back Stitch or the needle can be taken to the place where the next Detached Chain Stitch is to be formed.

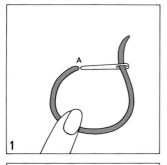

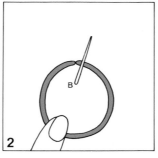

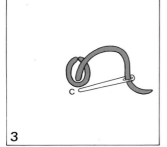

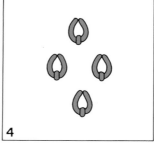

42

Leaf ▶

Ermine Filling

This simple stitch consists of a vertical strand crossed diagonally by two shorter strands. In the design on the opposite page, 'Carnation', the stitch is used for texturing the flower petals.

The shaded effect of the petals is worked with Long and Short Stitch, and the same stitch is used on the seed pod. Back Stitches and Stem Stitches are also used in the embroidery, together with Chain Stitch.

Stranded Cotton is used to work 'Carnation' as follows: 0894, 0893, 0895, 0896, 0897, 0215, 0216, 0217, 0218 and 0779.

Fig 1 *Bring the thread through at A and make a vertical stitch, inserting the needle at B. Bring the needle through at C diagonally down to the left of B.*

Fig 2 *Insert the needle at D, to the right and just above A, and make a small stitch under A-B to E.*

Fig 3 *Insert the needle at F, level with C and the same distance from the stitch A-B. This completes the cross.*

Fig 4 *This shows the effect of several Ermine Stitches worked as a filling.*

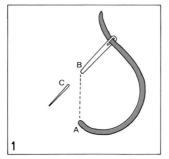

3

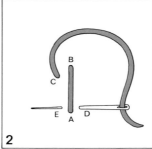

1

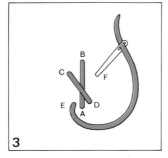

4

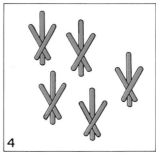

2

Carnation ▶
A trace-off pattern for this design is on page 108

44

Fern Stitch

Fern Stitch is often used for light foliage and tendrils in crewel work but in the design on the opposite page the stitch has been used for the bird's wing feathers. Other stitches in the embroidery are Chain Stitch, Satin Stitch, Stem Stitch, Detached Chain Stitches, French Knots and Pearl Stitch.

Fig 1 Bring the thread through at A and insert the needle at B.

Fig 2 Bring the needle through at C and insert it at A again.

Fig 3 Bring the thread through at D and insert the needle at A. The next group of stitches begins at E, below A (Fig 4).

Fig 5 and Fig 6 completes the group of stitches.

Parrot and Caterpillar ▶
A trace-off pattern for this design is on page 109

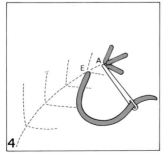

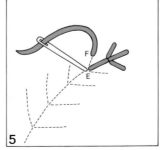

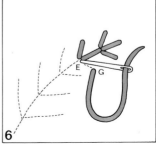

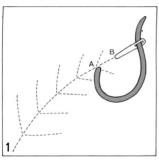

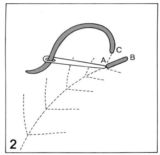

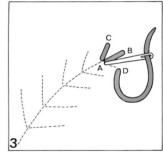

46

Fly Stitch, Single Attached

Fly Stitch is a looped stitch which can be used singly, as a scattered filling, in rows as a border, or as a close filling. The stitch has been used on the large flower in the design on the opposite page.

Tapisserie wool colours as follows: 0499, 0379, 0568, 0162, 0163, 067, 068, 0600, 0897. Stranded Cotton colours are 0390, 0378, 0936, and 0893.

Fig 1 Bring the thread through at A, hold it down with the thumb, insert the needle a little to the right at B and bring it through at C (midway between and below A-B)

Fig 2 Keeping the thread under the needle point, pull the thread through. Insert the needle at D to make a small tying stitch in the centre.

Fig 3 The finished stitch can be scattered as a filling.

Fig 4 Fly Stitches can also be worked in rows.

Fig 5 Here, Fly Stitches are worked one above the other. The width can be varied to fill a shape.

Blue and Brown ▶
A trace-off pattern for this design is on page 110

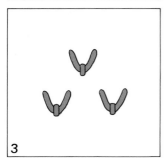

1

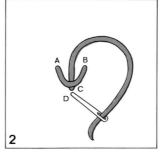

2

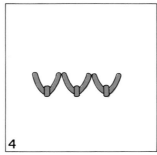

3

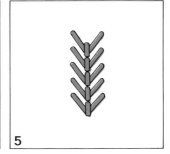

4

5

Four-legged Knot

The rose is one of the favourite flowers in crewel embroidery and takes many design forms. When used as an open-faced flower, it can be shown with alternating petals, as in the design on the opposite page. Sometimes, the flower is depicted with a small rose centred on a larger.

The design 'Open Rose' is worked in Stranded Cotton colours as follows: 0213, 0214, 0215, 0216, 0217, 0968, 0337, 0881, 08, 09 and 010.

Besides Four-legged Knots, used as a filling for the petals, Satin Stitch shading, Chain Stitch, Stem Stitch, Back Stitch, Long and Short Stitch and Half Fly Stitches are used.

Fig 1 *Bring the thread through at A and insert the needle at B a distance from A and below it. Bring the needle through at C half the distance of A-B to the right.*

Fig 2 *Pass the needle under the loop, then under stitch A-B, with the thread under the needle tip.*

Fig 3 *Insert the needle at D, half the distance between A-B to the left, to complete the knot.*

Fig 4 *Shows a group of knots worked.*

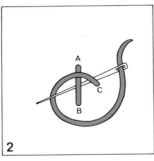

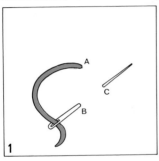

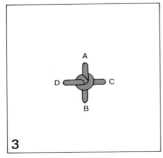

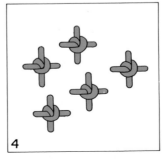

Open Rose ▶
A trace-off pattern for this design is on page 111

50

French Knot

Embroiderers used to enjoy embellishing their work with beasts and birds — and insects — and the colourful design opposite, Bird and Butterfly would make a charming framed picture. Alternatively, the design might be used with others featuring birds and insects, to decorate a large crewel wall hanging or curtain.

French Knots are massed for the bird's head and the butterfly's body while on the pink fruits, the Knots give way to Chain Stitches in the centres, suggesting roundness in the fruits and providing highlights.

Other stitches in the design are Satin Stitch, Stem Stitch Filling, Fly Stitches worked as a filling, Buttonhole Stitch and Back Stitch.

Fig 1 *Bring the thread through at A, the place where the Knot is to be positioned. Encircle the thread twice with the needle.*

Fig 2 *Holding the thread firmly with the thumb, twist the needle back to A and insert it close to where the thread first emerged.*

Fig 3 *Holding the Knot down with the thumb, pull*

the thread through at the back and secure it with a small stitch for a single French Knot.

Bird and Butterfly ▶
A trace-off pattern for this design is on page 112

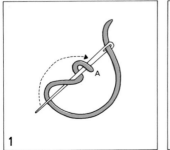

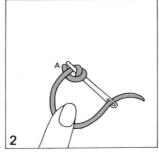

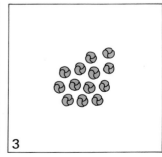

French Knots on Stalks

This variation on the French Knot produces a pretty, naturalistic effect in crewel when flower forms are depicted. It is particularly suited to the thistle flowers in the design opposite, but it also looks effective used for the daisy shape in the foreground. Used more freely, the stitch might also be used for flower forms such as dandelion clocks or for flying seeds.

A variety of stitches has been used in 'Thistles' as follows: Back Stitch, Stem Stitch, French Knots, Tied Trellis, Laid Satin, Filled Stem Stitch, Buttonhole Stitch, Roumanian Stitch and Chain Stitch.

Stranded Cotton is used for the embroidery, worked on a slub surfaced fabric, as follows: 095, 096, 0871, 0848, 0849, 0920, 0921, 0922, 0842, 0843, 0844, 0393 and 0392.

Fig 1 *Bring the thread through at A and encircle the thread twice with the needle.*

Fig 2 *Turn the needle point and insert into the fabric at the place the knot is to be positioned.*

Fig 3 *Pull the needle through to tighten the knot. To form a group of 'buds', bring the needle through at A again, ready to work the second French Knot on a Stalk. Work three, or as many as required.*

Thistles ▶
A trace-off pattern for this design is on page 113

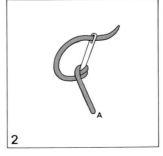

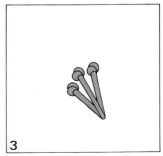

Closed Herringbone

The stag is one of the most-used animal motifs in crewel embroidery. The design on the opposite page is worked in Stranded Cotton.

Fig 1 Bring the thread through at A and insert the needle diagonally down to the right at B.

Fig 2 Bring the thread through at C and insert the needle at D to complete the cross.

Fig 3 Bring the thread through at E immediately beside A and insert the needle at F, beside B.

Fig 4 Bring the thread through at G, immediately beside C and insert the needle at H, immediately beside D.

Fig 5 Continue in this way to end of row.

Fig 6 By varying the length of the stitches, Close Herringbone can be worked to fill a shape.

Stag ▶

A trace-off pattern for this design is on page 114

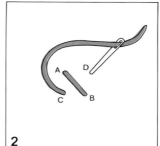

1

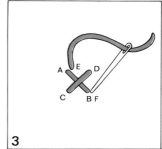

2

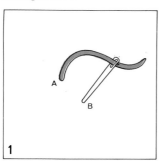

3

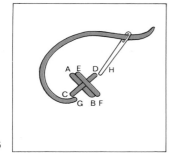

4

5

6

56

Honeycomb Filling

This attractive filling is one of the weaving stitches and is worked with three colour values for the best effect. In the design on the opposite page it is used to fill a large area of the design, the big, green leaf in the foreground. The design, 'Pomegranate' shows the fruit part-opened and displaying the seeds. The shape lends itself to versatility of treatment in stitches and the design is ideal for further development.

Stranded Cotton has been used for the design, colours as follows: 0185, 0390, 0391, 0392, 0393, 0842, 0843, 0844, 0881, 0882 and 0878.

Stitches used in the design include Stem and Chain Stitches, Satin Stitch, Long and Short Stitch, French Knots and Filled Stem Stitch.

Fig 1 *Work the foundation rows first, working stitches A-B, C-D, E-F, G-H, I-J, K-L. Stitches E-F and G-H are the same length. Keep stitches equidistantly spaced.*

Fig 2 *For the second stage, work diagonal stitches across the foundation rows as shown. Bring the thread through one-third along and below K-L and insert the needle just above G. Continue working parallel stitches, keeping them equidistantly spaced.*

Fig 3 *To complete the filling, weave the needle through the crossed rows of stitches, under the foundation rows and over the stage two diagonal stitches.*

Pomegranate ▶
A trace-off pattern for the design is on page 115

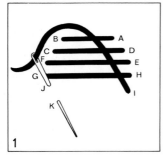

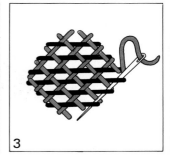

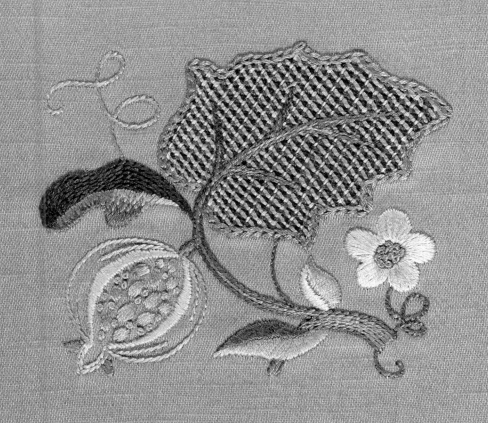

Laid Work

Laid work is one of the quickest ways of filling design areas. In traditional crewel designs, laid work is often used for tree branches and large leaves but in the design 'Strawberries' on the opposite page, the technique has been used for the mound.

Long Satin Stitches have been used for two of the leaves, the veins couched in contrasting colours, while other leaves are worked in Satin Stitch and Stem Stitch Filling.

Fig 1 *Lay a strand of thread from left to right along the base of the design area (A-B).*

Fig 2 *Continue laying threads to follow the design line as shown.*

Fig 3 *With a contrasting thread, come through at A and insert the needle at B immediately below.*
Work C-D close beside A-B.

Work groups of 2 stitches in the same way across the laid threads, keeping the spaces between the groups the same (E-F, G-H, I-J, K-L).

Fig 4 *Work small horizontal tying stitches across the vertical threads.*

Fig 5 *The finished effect of the stitch.*

Strawberries ▶
A trace-off pattern for this design is on page 116

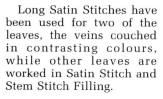

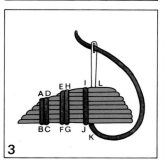

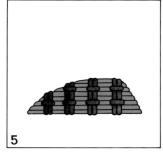

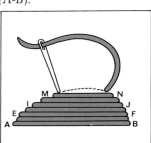

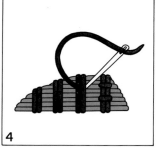

60

Long and Short Stitch

Long and Short Stitches are sometimes used when a colour shaded effect is required. The Stitch produces a smooth, lustrous effect when Stranded Cottons are used.

Fig 1 *Bring the needle through at A and insert it at B. To make the next, longer stitch, bring the needle through at C.*

Fig 2 *Insert the needle at D,* close beside B and bring it out at E.

Continue in this way.

Fig 3 *To work the second row, bring the needle through at G and insert it at H, bringing it out again at I.*

Fig 4 *Continue as shown.*

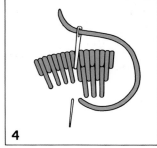

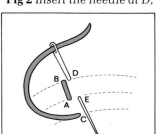

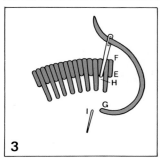

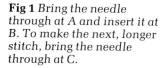

Pomegranate ▶

Moss Stitch

The flower and leaf design on the opposite page is worked in Tapisserie wools in two sets of colour values — blues and blue greens, and a range of soft brown tones. These are traditional colours for crewel embroideries and 'Blue Motif' is an ideal repeat design for a large piece of work such as a door curtain or a wall hanging.

Moss Stitch is used as a scattered filling for the large flower-like form in the middle of the embroidery, together with Seeding, Satin Stitch, French Knots, Pearl Stitch, Stem Stitch Filling, Back and Chain Stitches.

Fig 1 *Bring the thread through at A and insert it at B diagonally opposite. Bring the needle through at C.*

Fig 2 *From C, complete a cross by inserting the needle at D, bring the needle through at E, midway between A and D and above.*

Fig 3 *From E, form a loop. Hold the thread down with the thumb and pass the needle under the thread between E-D.*

Fig 4 *Turn the needle back over the thread, then pass under the crossed threads.*

Fig 5 *Insert the needle at F to complete the stitch.*
Blue Motif▶

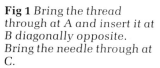

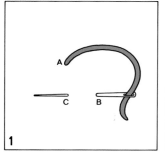

1

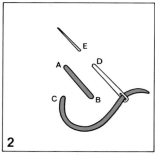

2

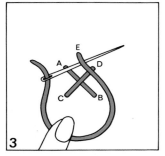

3

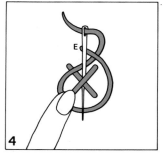

4

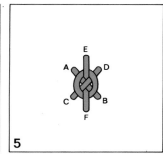

5

Pearl Stitch

The design opposite is another interpretation of a crewel pomegranate motif, worked in Stranded Cotton which lends a lustrous, three-dimensional effect. Colours used are 049, 076, 077, 078, 0108, 0109, 0110, 0111, 0388, 0392 and 0393.

Rows of Pearl Stitch have been used in the pomegranate shapes and to outline the pink leaf on the right. Satin Stitches and French Knots are used in the design together with Chain Stitch, Stem Stitch and Back Stitch.

Pearl Stitch Knots can be closely spaced or set wide apart as required.

Fig 1 Bring the thread through at A and insert it at B immediately above. Bring the needle through at C, level with B.

Fig 2 From C, insert the needle under the thread A-B.

Fig 3 Pull through to set the knot, then insert the needle the required distance above at D, ready to make the next stitch. Work D-E as for B-C in Figs 1 and 2.

Fig 4 shows the row of Pearl Stitches.

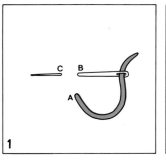

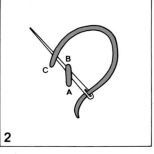

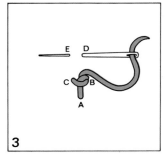

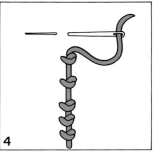

Pink Pomegranates ▶
A trace-off pattern for this design is on page 117

Pekin Knot

This attractive stitch is useful when a more textured outlining stitch is needed and the effect can be seen in 'Blue Fruit' on the opposite page where the stitch is used to outline some of the leaves.

This charming motif would be ideal for working on personal accessories such as a small bag or a book cover, although it would be equally effective as a repeat on a larger piece of embroidery. The design might also be used as a corner motif on a cushion or on a firescreen.

The design is worked in Stranded Cotton, colours as follows: 0120, 0121, 0122, 0123, 0167, 0168, 0372, 0373, and 0375.

Other stitches in the design are Satin Stitch, Stem Stitch, Long and Short Stitch, Trellis (using 0123 and 0373), and Back Stitch.

French Knots are used massed together to form the small seed heads.

Fig 1 *Working right to left, bring the thread through at A, hold the loop of thread down with the thumb and pass the needle under the loop.*

Fig 2 *Still holding the loop, insert the needle at B,* *inside the loop of the thread and bring it out at C, just below B.*

Fig 3 *Pull the thread gently to set the knot, form and hold the loop of thread as in Fig 1 and insert the needle again as in Fig 2.*

Blue Fruit ▶

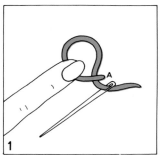

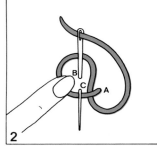

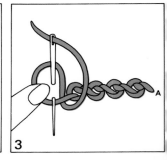

Plate Stitch

This stitch produces a close texture and is used in the design opposite 'Little Hill', to work the hill at the bottom of the design. Three shades of green Tapisserie wool have been used, 0240, 0265 and 0266.

Both Tapisserie wool and Stranded Cottons are used in the embroidery, the Stranded Cotton (colour 0894) being used for the lighter flower effects and for the little snail's body.

Fig 1 Bring the thread through at A and insert it at B a short distance below A. Bring the needle through at C, below B and a little to the right and insert it again at D, immediately above and just above B.

Fig 2 Two stitches having been set, continue working E-F as A-B.

Fig 3 To move to the subsequent row, work G-H as shown, then pass the needle from H to I.

Fig 4 Work I-J as A-B. If you want to continue the stitch to fill a design area, from J, bring the needle through at K, inserting it again at L, to the right of and just above J.

Fig 5 Shows the effect of the stitch.

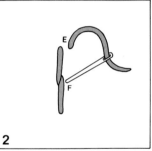

1

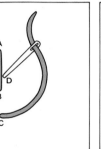

2

Little Hill ▶

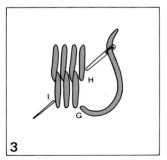

3

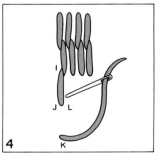

4

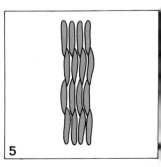

5

70

Roumanian Stitch

This stitch is also known as Roumanian Couching and uses the same thread for the laid thread and the couching. Stitches can be worked to varying lengths to fill a shape, such as the leaves in the design 'Pale Rose' opposite.

Fig 1 Bring the thread through at A, insert the needle at B bring it out at C.

Fig 2 Insert the needle at D on the design line and bring it out at E, keeping thread under needle.

Fig 3 Insert the needle at F and bring it out at G.

Fig 4 Insert the needle at H and bring it out at I.

Fig 5 Insert the needle at J and bring it out at K.

Fig 6 Continue working in this sequence.

Pale Rose ▶
A trace-off pattern for this design is on page 118

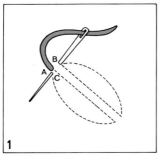

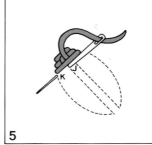

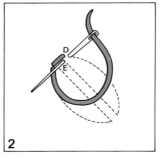

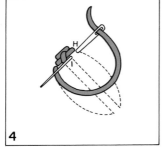

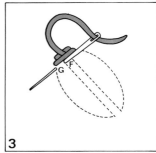

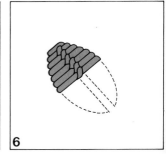

Satin Stitch

Satin Stitch is a suitable stitch for filling in the solid areas of a design and, although basically very simple to work, it takes practice to get the surface smooth and the edges even.

The stitch is used extensively in the design on the opposite page, 'Summer Flowers', with Back Stitches used for the tendrils, and Buttonhole Stitch flowers. French Knots are used for the rabbit's tail and for outlining one of the mounds. Note the snail creeping along a petal, and a bird of almost the same size clinging to a tendril. Trellis (in Stranded Cotton colours 0108 and 085) is worked in the centre of the largest flower.

Fig 1 *Bring the thread through at A and insert the needle at B.*

Fig 2 *Bring the needle out at C, close to A.*

Fig 3 *Insert the needle at D, close to B.*

Fig 4 *Continue in sequence, placing stitches close together so that no background fabric shows through and keeping the edges of the shape even and neat.*

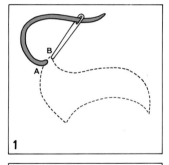

1

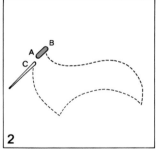

2

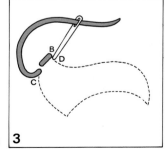

3

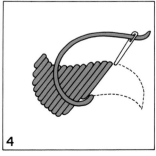

4

Summer Flowers ▶
A trace-off pattern for this design is on page 119

74

Satin Fan Block Shading

Satin Fan Block Shading consists of Satin Stitches working in rows, the effect being achieved by using graduating shades of thread or yarn. This can be seen in the tree trunk of the tree in 'Fawn' on the opposite page. Stranded Cotton colours 0936, 0378, 0347, 0349 and 0352 are used.

The design would make a charming framed picture, worked on a finely woven cream wool fabric or the motif could be matched to others of similar style and colour, repeated over a larger piece of embroidery.

A grey snail can be seen creeping through the grass in the foreground while a bluebird flies blithely by.

Trellis (in colours 0850 and 0832), Long and Short Stitch, Chain Stitch and French Knots are also used in the design.

Fig 1 *Bring the thread through at A and work Satin Stitches of the same length close together between the design lines at the base of the fan shape. Work A-B, C-D, E-F.*

Fig 2 *Changing to a deeper shade, work Satin Stitches between the design lines,*

keeping stitches close together and to exactly the same length.

Fig 3 *Work each row of Satin Stitches in the same way, progressing thread colours from light to dark, and working to the shape of the fan.*

Fawn ▶
A trace-off pattern for this design is on page 120

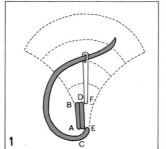

1

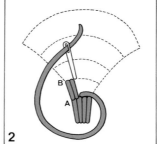

2

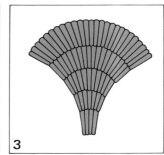

3

Knotted Satin Stitch

This unusual stitch is worked in a similar way to Satin Stitch but a knot is formed at the lower edge of each stitch, slightly lifting the edge. The stitch has been used for the large bronze petals in the design 'Bronze Flower' on the opposite page. Trellis is used to fill these petals in Stranded Cotton colours 0365 and 0363, tied down with 0361. As a texture contrast, small flowers have been worked in Satin Stitch and French Knots, with small leaves in Cretan Stitch. Other leaves are outlined in Back Stitch.

Stranded Cotton in the following colours is used for the embroidery: 0886, 0887, 0888, 0906, 0361, 0362, 0363, 0365, 0336, 0338, 011, 09 and 06.

Stitches include Trellis, Satin Stitch, French Knots, Chain Stitch, Cretan Stitch, Stem Stitch, Detached Chain Stitches and Coral Stitch.

Fig 1 *Bring the thread through at A, insert it at B immediately above and bring it out close to A with the thread under the needle.*

Fig 2 *Draw the thread through and insert the needle immediately above*

next to B, and bring the needle through close to the last stitch with the thread under the needle.

Fig 3 *Continue in the same way.*

Bronze Flower ▶

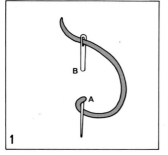
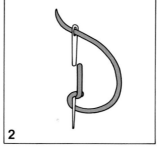
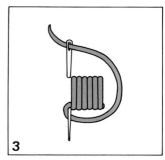

78

Satin Threaded Chain Stitch

This stitch is worked in two stages. First, a row of Chain Stitch is worked along the design line. In the next stage, Satin Stitches are threaded through the Chain Stitch loops.

The effect can be seen outlining the lily shape in the design on the opposite page. For textural contrast, Chain Stitch Filling in shaded tones is worked on the largest leaf, with outlining in Stem Stitch. The tree trunk is worked in Long and Short Stitches, the stitches angled towards the centre so that the trunk has a rounded look. Small flowers are worked in Buttonhole Stitch and Satin Stitch.

Stranded Cotton in the following colours is used to work the embroidery: 0366, 0942, 0374, 0375, 0875, 0876, 0878, 0869, 0870 and 0871.

Fig 1 *Work a row of Chain Stitch. From the right, bring the thread through at A and pass the needle through the loop of the first chain (B).*

Fig 2 *Take a small Running Stitch beside A (C-D) and pass the needle through the next chain above.*

Fig 3 *Continue in the same way, following the design line.*

Blue Lily ▶
A trace-off pattern for this design is on page 121

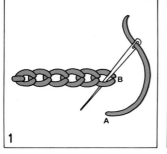

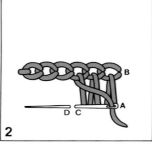

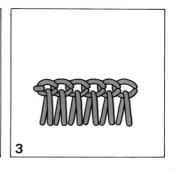

Seeding

This is a popular and easily-worked stitch and can be scattered as an open filling or grouped in tight clusters. The stitches can be set at different angles, or, if you prefer, can lie in one direction.

In the design on the opposite page 'Eden', Seeding can be seen filling the upper leaves of the branch.

Serpents and snakes are sometimes used in crewel design, usually with apple motifs, to symbolise the triumph of Satan over man. In this design, the serpent winds itself up the branch, with a green butterfly passing by.

The Stranded Cotton colours are as follows: 0253, 0254, 0266, 0376, 0378, 0842, 0843 and 0845.

Stitches include Long and Short Stitch, Stem Stitch, Satin Stitch, Open Herringbone and French Knots.

Fig 1 *Bring the thread through at A and make a small straight stitch, inserting the needle at B.*

Fig 2 *From B, bring the needle through a short distance away at an angle from B, inserting the needle to complete the second Seeding stitch.*

Fig 3 *Shows the massed effect of Seeding stitches set at different angles.*

Eden ▶
A trace-off pattern for this design is on page 122

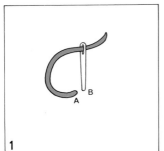

1

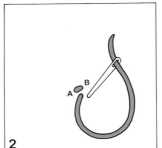

2

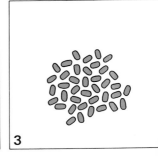

3

Sheaf or Faggot Stitch

The finished stitch looks like a tied bundle of wheat (or faggots) and is worked by passing the thread twice round groups of straight stitches.

Stitches can be worked in alternate rows (as in the design 'Rabbit at Rest' on the opposite page) or can be set in a line with the ends touching.

Fig 1 Lay 3 straight stitches, A-B, C-D and E-F, and bring out at G.

Fig 2 Pass the thread round the stitches once without piercing the fabric, taking care not to pull the thread too tightly.

Fig 3 Insert the needle at J.

Fig 4 shows the finished effect.

Fig 5 Longer stitches in groups of 5 makes a variation. Try tying sheaves with thread of a different colour (Fig 6)

Rabbit at Rest ▶
A trace-off pattern for this design is on page 123

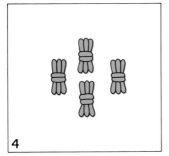

1

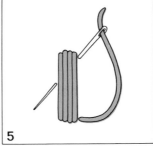

2

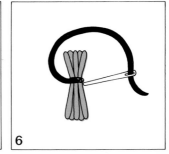

3

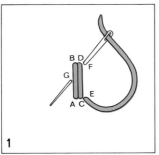

4

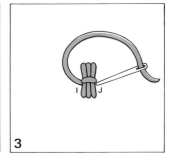

5

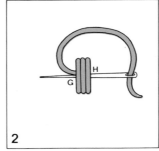

6

Stem Outline and Filling

Stem Stitch shows its versatility in this example of crewel embroidery. The vine-wrapped branch is worked in rows of Stem Stitch and so are the leaves crossing the branch. Both mixed-tone leaves are detailed with Stem Stitch and the cluster of grapes is also worked in Stem Stitch.

Stitches include Satin Stitch, Stem Filling and Straight Stitch arrowheads.

Fig 1 *Bring the thread through on the design line at A and hold it down with the thumb. Insert the needle at B and bring it out at C, midway between A and B.*

Fig 2 *Pull the thread through to set the first stitch. Hold the working thread down with the thumb and insert the needle at D, bringing it out at B.*

Fig 3 *Insert the needle at E and bring it out at D. Continue in this way, making each stitch exactly the same length.*

Fig 4 *The effect of the stitch.*

Fig 5 *shows the effect when used as a filling.*

Grapes ▶
A trace-off pattern for this design is on page 124

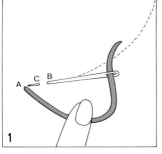

1

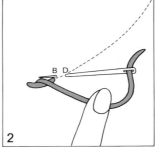

2

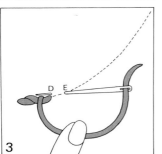

3

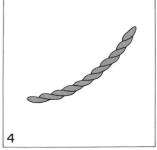

4

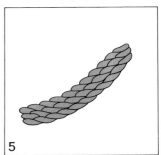

5

Portuguese Knotted Stem Stitch

Fig 1 Bring the thread through at A and insert it at B immediately above, making a vertical straight stitch. Bring the needle through at C, midway between A and B.

Fig 2 Make a tying stitch round A-B (C-D) without piercing the fabric and bring the needle out at E.

Fig 3 From E, make another tying stitch round A-B, (E-F). Bring the needle out at G.

Fig 4 From G, insert the needle above B at H, bringing it out again to the left of B.

Fig 5 Make a tying stitch round the A-B and G-H threads.

Fig 6 Make a second tying stitch as in Fig 3, then proceed to position of next stitch as shown.

Blue Moon Flower ▶

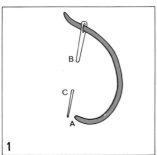

1

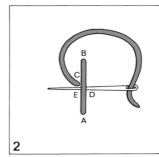

2

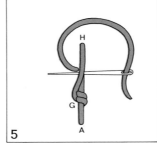

3

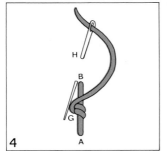

4

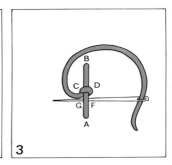

5

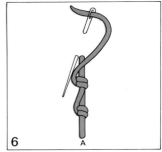

6

Tête de Boeuf

These stitches are worked as a chunky filling in the flower form in the design 'Peony' on the opposite page.

The stitch is formed by working two straight stitches at an angle to each other, in a V-shape, then a loop is formed over the stitches.

The loop is then tied at the bottom.

The design is worked in Tapisserie wools, colours as follows: 3285, 0842, 3087 0638, 0604, 0869, 0870, 0605, 3154, 095, 0502 and 0872.

Fig 1 Bring the thread through at A and make a short diagonal stitch to B.

Fig 2 Bring the thread through at C and make a short diagonal stitch towards B but not actually touching it (D).

Fig 3 From D, bring the needle through at E, between the two diagonal stitches. Holding the loop of thread with the thumb, insert needle again at E and bring out at F, a short distance below, keeping thread under needle.

Fig 4 Tighten stitch gently and insert the needle at G to tie the loop.

Fig 5 shows three Tête de Boeuf Stitches.

Peony ▶

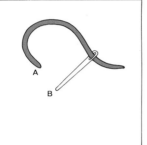

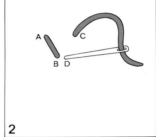

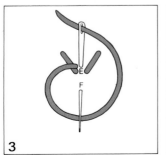

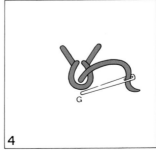

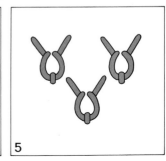

Thorn Stitch

Fig 1 Shows the formation of the stitch.

Fig 2 Lay the thread A-B, bringing the thread through to the right side at C, to the right of A-B. Insert the needle at D, to the left of A-B.

Fig 3 Bring the thread through at E, level with C and insert it at F, level with D.

Fig 4 From F, bring the needle through at G, level with the crossed threads and insert the needle at H, below D.

Fig 5 From H, bring the thread through at I, level with the crossed threads and insert the needle at J, making the second cross.

Fig 6 Shows the effect of the stitch.

Thorn Flower ▶
A trace-off pattern for this design is on page 125

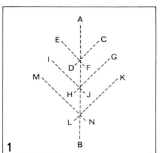

1

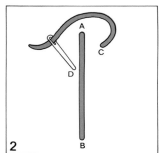

2

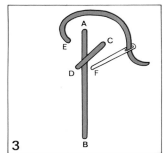

3

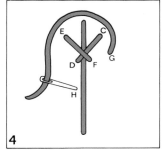

4

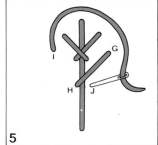

5

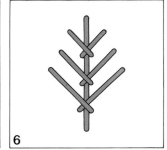

6

Trellis Square Filling

Fig 1 Lay a foundation of threads, A-B, C-D, E-F and G-H.

Fig 2 Work vertical threads over the horizontal threads, I-J, K-L, M-N and O-P.

Fig 3 Work small diagonal tying stitches over each intersection.

Fig 4 Is a variation where diagonal threads have been laid and then tying stitches worked over the intersections of 4 threads and 2 threads.

Fig 5 In this variation, long Cross Stitches are worked over the intersections of 4 threads and tying stitches over 2 threads.

Fig 6 Shows a simple Trellis with tying stitches worked over the intersections with a French Knot or Detached Chain Stitch worked in each square.

Autumn Fruit ►
A trace-off pattern for this design is on page 126

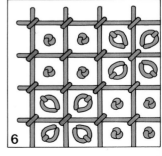

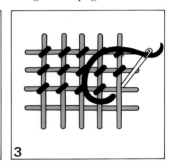

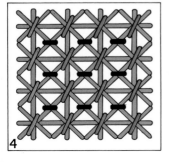

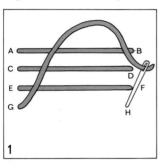

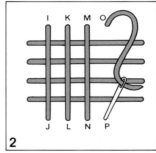

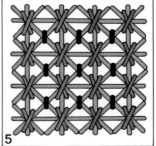

Wave Stitch

This makes a honeycomb pattern and, depending on the spacing, the effect can be rather closed, or open and lacey as in the design on the opposite page.

The stitch is easy to work and areas can be filled quite quickly.

Stranded Cotton has been used for the embroidery in the following colours: 0387, 0899, 0903, 0905, 0849, 0850, 0779, 0851, 0842, 0843, 0844, 0259, 0260, 0261 and 0262.

Stitches include Close Buttonhole Stitch, French Knots, Long and Short Stitch, Stem Stitch, Satin Stitch and Chain Stitch.

Fig 1 Work a row of small vertical Satin stitches, evenly spaced.

Fig 2 Bring the thread through at A on the lower design line, and pass the needle through the first Satin Stitch.

Fig 3 From B, make a small Running Stitch on the design line at C-D.

Fig 4 Continue passing threads through the vertical Satin Stitches to form a row of Wave Stitches. The second row passes the thread through the stitch bases of the previous row.

Fig 5 Subsequent rows are worked in the same way.

◀ **Seedhead**
A trace-off pattern for this design is on page 127

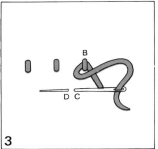

1

2

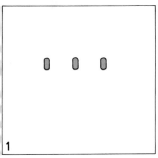

3

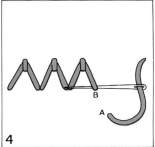

4

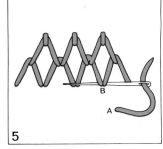

5

Flower Tree
page 27

Flower and Snail
page 33

105

Carnation
page 45

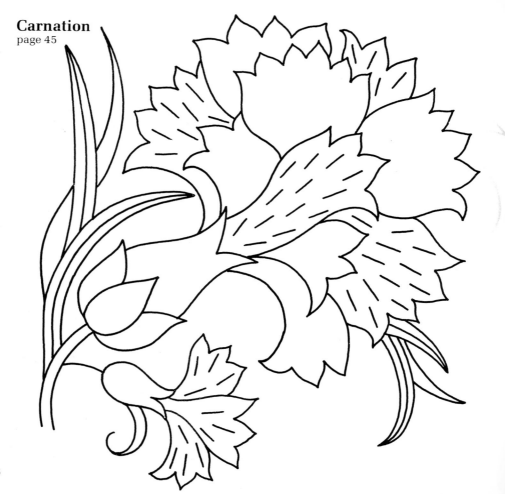

Blue and Brown
page 49

Open Rose
page 51

Bird and Butterfly
page 53

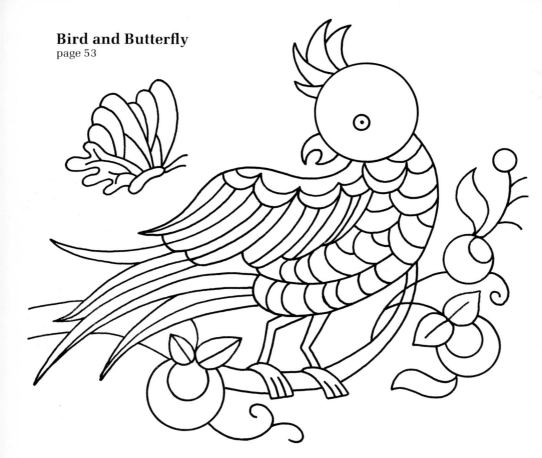

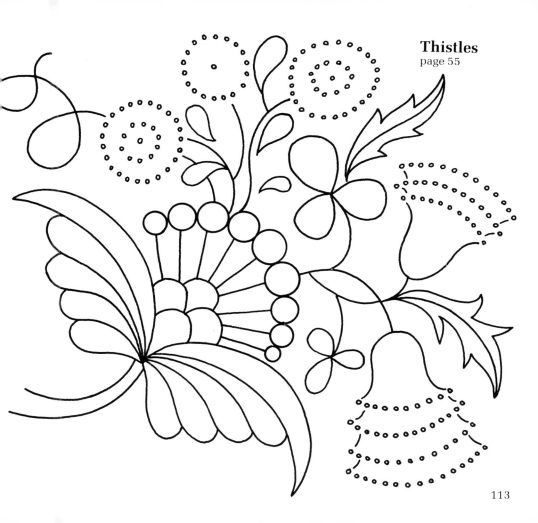

Thistles
page 55

Stag
page 57

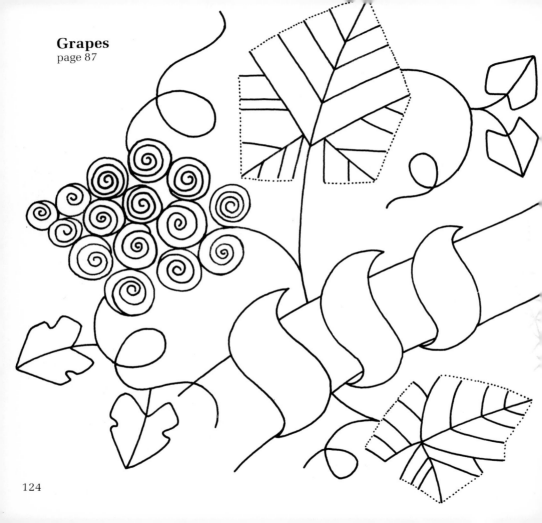

Grapes
page 87

124

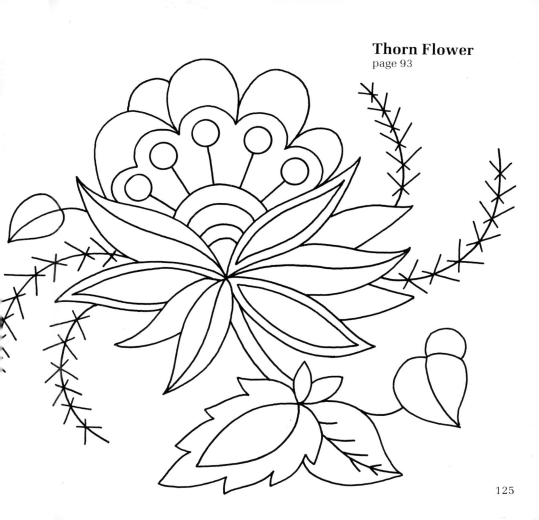

Autumn Fruit

page 95

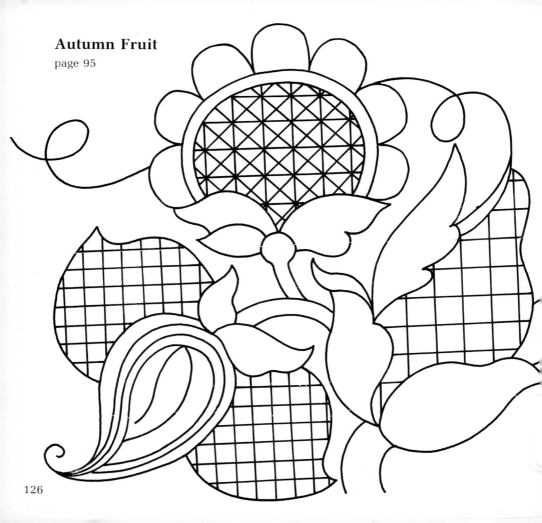

Seedhead
page 96

Thread, Needle and Fabric Guide

Fabric	Anchor Embroidery threads	Strand thickness	Milward International Range Needle sizes		
			Tapestry Needles (rounded points)		
Fine evenweave fabric	Stranded Cotton Pearl Cotton No. 8, 5 Coton à Broder No. 16	1–6	No.	Strand thickness 1 and 2 strands	
			24	3 strands, Coton à Broder No. 16	
Medium weight evenweave fabric, medium mesh canvas, etc.	Stranded Cotton Pearl Cotton No. 8, 5 Coton à Broder No. 16 Tapisserie Wool	3, 4 or 6		4 strands, Pearl Cotton No. 8	
			20	6 strands, Pearl Cotton No. 5	
			18	Soft Embroidery, Tapisserie Wool	
Coarse or heavy evenweave fabric, heavy mesh canvas, etc.	Stranded Cotton Pearl Cotton No. 5 Soft Embroidery Tapisserie Wool	4 or 6			
Medium weight square weave canvas	Stranded Cotton Pearl Cotton No. 5 Soft Embroidery Tapisserie Wool	3, 4 or 6	No. 20 18	Strand thickness 6 strands, Pearl Cotton No. 5 Soft Embroidery, Tapisserie Wool	
Heavy square weave canvas	Stranded Cotton Soft Embroidery Tapisserie Wool	6			

British Library Cataloguing in Publication Data

Harlow, Eve
The new Anchor book of crewel embroidery stitches and patterns
1. Crewel embroidery – Manuals
I. Title
746.44

ISBN 0-7153-9185-2

First published 1989
Reprinted 1990, 1991, 1992, 1993, 1995

Printed in Italy by New Interlitho for David & Charles plc
Brunel House   Newton Abbot   Devon